HENLEY
the regatta

To mark the 150th anniversary of the Henley Royal Regatta, the world's foremost rowing festival, we publish this brilliant photographic study by Roger George Clark and Daniel Topolski. It perfectly captures the spirit of the event – not just the tension and excitement of the rowing, the near-collisions, the exhaustion of the crews as they come up to the finish, their utter elation when they win, but also the quintessentially English atmosphere of an Edwardian garden party that surrounds it all. Henley may have moved with the times, attracting more international crews and greater crowds every year, but it has never cut loose from tradition and expresses all the hedonism of a former age: the Pimms, the picnics, and elegant spectators looking on from their punts, the strains of the band from the Stewards' Enclosure – not even incessant rain and the ensuing mudbath could spoil the fun in 1988.

Roger George Clark has been taking photographs for twenty years, and has photographed Henley for five. His work is in the National Portrait Gallery and has been shown at the National Theatre, and he writes and broadcasts regularly on photography. He worked in publishing and at the *Observer* before joining the BBC, where he works full-time as a producer and broadcaster.

Daniel Topolski, a first-class oarsman himself, coached the Oxford Boat Race team for fifteen years, guiding the Dark Blues through their longest-running winning streak. He is the author of *Boat Race*, and *True Blue*, an account of the Oxford Mutiny.

HENLEY
the regatta

PHOTOGRAPHS BY
ROGER GEORGE CLARK

TEXT BY
DANIEL TOPOLSKI

JOHN
MURRAY

To my friend and fellow broadcaster Tom Boswell,
Chairman of Leander Club, who helped to make this
book possible.

Roger George Clark

First published 1989
Copyright in the photographs © Roger George Clark 1989
Copyright in the text © Daniel Topolski 1989
Text and cover designed by Peartree Design Associates
Printed and bound in Great Britain by
Butler & Tanner Ltd, Frome and London
British Library Cataloguing in Publication Data
Topolski, Daniel
Henley: the Regatta.
1. Oxfordshire. Henley-on-Thames. Thames
river. Rowing boats. Racing. Regattas: Henley
Royal Regatta, to 1988
I. Title II. Clark, Roger George
797.1′4′09422579

ISBN 0–7195–4719–9

HENLEY ROYAL REGATTA

The Henley Experience

Henley Royal Regatta goes from strength to strength. As the current Stewards look back over its 150-year history they can feel proud both to have upheld the values and traditions of this world-famous event and to have moved with the times. In the 1970s Henley's finances were shaky and its future uncertain. Now the Regatta is profitable and draws ever larger crowds.

For many, Henley's main function is to provide a riverside setting for those enjoying the 'London season'. For the Chairman of the Regatta Committee of Management, Peter Coni, QC, OBE, the rowing comes first but for some, he suggests, 'it is a nice, informal but genteel Edwardian garden party with rowing going on at the edge of the lawn'. As June gives way to July the Regatta takes its place after Ascot and before Wimbledon Finals day and

Cowes. Without Henley there would be an embarrassing gap in the summer's social merry-go-round and poor Wimbledon would have to take up the slack.

But if Henley is a must for London's bright young things, it represents Mecca for the world's rowing fraternity. Whatever their standard, the chance for oarsmen to row on the same stretch of water and against some of the world's best crews is thrilling. Just to take part is special. And this is as true for oarsmen from Russia, America, Egypt, Italy and East Germany as it is for those from Putney, Newcastle, Oxford or East Grinstead.

Astonishingly, this eccentric but uniquely British affair serves as a magnet for the very best of world rowing. They all want to row, and if possible win, at Henley at least once in their lives. It is one thing doing the international regatta circuit and the Olympics, with their

custom-built, six-lane, still-water 2000-metre courses, all regularly buoyed and boasting the best high-tech timing systems to show 1/100th of a second difference between Gold and oblivion. But there is nothing in the world like Henley's two-lane knockout competition, racing between two sets of solid wooden booms connecting those unforgiving upright stakes which have been the undoing of many an inexperienced steersman. The curious race distance of 1 mile 550 yards has also caught quite a few international experts napping.

At Henley there are no second chances as there are through the international 'repechage' system, and the verdicts are still given traditionally as a 'canvas' or in feet, lengths, and 'Easily'. Then there is all that gloriously elaborate presentation silverware to be won. And in the Stewards' Enclosure gentlemen still have to wear jacket and tie, while ladies in slacks or above-the-knee mini-skirts are refused entry. What an extraordinary atmosphere there is along the banks and in the Enclosure, where sometimes the impression is that hardly anyone watches the racing! What a pleasure for visiting Russian teams to see the profusion of boaters and the frocks and the college blazers punting by. Could *glasnost* bring a little of this panache to future regattas on the Volga?

Rowing – A Growing Sport

These days, as more and more rowers take up the sport and yearn to compete at the Regatta, even getting through the qualifying rounds on the Friday before the start is something to be proud of. More than a quarter of the British entries will have been eliminated by the time the first day of racing gets under way. They will not even make the draw. Only the very best British crews and foreign entrants can count on getting a place in the Regatta proper.

So if the ever-increasing numbers wanting to take part are anything to go by – and the Regatta Stewards have had to extend the programme to five days to make room for them – then Henley more than justifies its existence.

First Stirrings

Except during the period of the two world wars, the Henley Regatta has been held every year since 1839, becoming 'Royal' in 1851 when Prince Albert became its first royal patron. Since then the reigning sovereign has always agreed to take on the role.

The success of the first Oxford and Cambridge Boat Race, which took place on the Henley reach in 1829, and a number of subsequent aquatic contests, inspired the local mayor and the townspeople to establish a regular amateur rowing event along with a fair and other popular entertainments. This they felt 'under judicious and respectable management would not only be productive of the most beneficial results to the town, but from its peculiar attractions would also be a source of amusement and gratification to the neighbourhood and the public in general'.

There were that year races in eights for the Grand Challenge Cup, in fours for the Town Challenge Cup and a special race for watermen. The contestants in eights came wholly from Oxford and Cambridge. First Trinity Boat Club, Cambridge was the first name to grace the Grand, defeating the Oxford Etonians to earn that distinction. It has been claimed that Leander, while declining to take part, rowed alongside the racing crews, having paddled all the way upriver from London.

The experiment proved such an attraction that within eight years a one-day three-event regatta had blossomed into a two-day, eleven-event extravaganza. It did not become a three-day regatta until 1886 and ran for four days from 1906.

Foreign Invaders

The first foreigner, E. Smith from New York, entered the Diamond Sculls in 1872, followed six years later by the first overseas crews. These were Columbia University, USA, who won the Visitors' Fours and the Shoe-wae-cae-mette Boat Club from Canada who lost the final of the Stewards'. The French/Canadians were rather frowned upon because they appeared to be 'working men' and finely trained, rowing at a very high rate of striking. Ruffled Henley feathers were soothed, however, when they failed to take the prize.

It was not until 1906 that the Regatta's top prize, the Grand, went overseas, won by the Belgian crew Club Nautique de Gand. Since then it has left these shores 30 times, including nine times to the USSR (since the Russians' first victorious visit in 1954) and nine to America – five of which were to Harvard. Two years after the Belgian triumph, the 1908 Olympic Regatta was held over the Henley course, an occasion repeated for the 1948

Olympic Games.

The Stewards' Enclosure was first opened in 1919 on the occasion of the Peace Regatta and the present straight course was introduced in 1924. It was not until 1938, however, that the notoriously restrictive 'manual labour' rule was finally lifted. This regulation was said to have barred Grace Kelly's father John from competing in the Diamond Sculls because, it was alleged, he had in his youth been an apprentice bricklayer and was therefore considered ineligible. His son Jack, Grace's brother, avenged that slight by returning with his father in 1947 to win the Diamonds instead. To underline the point he won again in 1949.

Thirty-two years later, perhaps further to demonstrate that the Kellys had decided to let bygones be bygones, Grace Kelly agreed to present the prizes at the 1981 Regatta. On the last day she followed one of the greatest races ever seen at Henley, the final of the Grand between Oxford University/Thames Tradesmen and the British National crew. It was the Dark Blues' first win in the Grand for 128 years, although many Oxford men had won the event over the years, rowing under various other titles.

Recent Changes

Since the war a number of new events have been introduced into the Regatta programme. The Princess Elizabeth Cup for school eights was held in 1946 for the first time while events for coxed fours had to wait another 17 years. The Prince Philip Cup presented for crews of international standard in 1963 was followed in 1968 by the Britannia Cup for domestic coxed fours. Next came the Special Race for Schools in 1974, held over a shortened course and restricted to the Saturday and Sunday of the Regatta to accommodate 'A' level examinees. The last addition to the 14-strong programme of events was the Queen Mother Cup for Quadruple Sculls in 1981, arguably the most harmonious and elegant of all racing shells. Only a top-class eight is faster.

In 1981 the Henley Stewards also launched an experimental programme of racing for women on an invitation basis, although lady coxswains in men's crews had been permitted since 1975. The idea was judged a success by many with crews from Canada, Europe and the United States competing with the best that Britain could offer in fours, double sculls and singles. But the experiment was discontinued,

with a final decision on their permanent participation being postponed indefinitely. In the meantime, Britain's oarswomen established their own Henley Regatta in 1988 which took place in mid-June. The Henley Stewards are said to be still deeply divided on whether to embrace women wholeheartedly on the hallowed Royal Regatta course.

Most recently the magnificent new Headquarters building next to Henley bridge was opened by the Queen in the spring of 1986. This was also the year that the Regatta mounted a five-day programme for the first time, reflecting perhaps the biggest surge in its popularity this century. Two years later Temple Island, the historic landmark built by James Wyatt in 1771 that stands at the start of the Regatta course, came onto the market. The Stewards were determined that they should somehow secure the island for the Regatta so that they could control its future use.

At the eleventh hour a benefactor appeared in the form of Henley Steward Alan Burrough, a former Cambridge Blue. Having recently sold his interest in the family business, Beefeater Gin, sponsors of that other great rowing institution, the Oxford and Cambridge Boat Race, he and his wife Rosie decided that Temple Island must be delivered to the Royal Regatta, and the deal was done. The Stewards set about restoring the Temple and its Etruscan-style murals so that it could be used as an exclusive enclosure for Stewards' members and their guests.

Nuts and Bolts

Since 1884 the organisation of the Regatta has been in the hands of a self-electing group of fifty or so Stewards, men who at some time in their careers have performed with distinction in the sport of rowing. With their practical experience they are clearly the best-qualified people to run the Regatta and now a twelve-strong management committee is elected every year.

Angus Robertson was made a Henley Steward in 1976 although his distinctive voice has been heard leading the race commentary team over the Enclosure loudspeaker system since 1964. His ability to master the most complicated overseas club and competitors' names invariably elicits a round of spontaneous applause from racegoers. He is a consultant engineer by profession but admits that

whenever there is a conflict of interests his Henley duties receive first call.

'There is no doubt that our purple patch has been the last ten years,' he says. 'The standard of the winners has rocketed, there has been a vast increase in membership with over 100,000 visitors over five days and the number of entries has risen from a steady 250 to an anticipated 500 or more for the 150th anniversary regatta, a fifth of whom will be from abroad.'

Mr Robertson remembers his unhappiest moment as the day he had to tell the representative of the Norwegian club Christiana Roklub, who had flown in especially to register his crew's entry, that his efforts were in vain. Rules could not be changed and their entry had arrived too late. 'But the most exciting race for me was the 1981 Grand final when Oxford rowed down the National squad from nearly a length behind . . . oh! and of course 1988's defeat of the Australian Olympic eight.'

The Henley Stewards all give freely of their time. 'We need people with full commitment to the sport because we are, after all, running the best regatta in the world.' And he adds: 'It has given me more pleasure than I could ever have dreamt of.'

A Word from the Chairman

'It ought to get simpler every year as we become more efficient,' muses Peter Coni, Chairman of the Regatta and a QC in his spare time, 'but it doesn't. It gets harder because there is so much more to be done – logistics, more crews, more facilities, extra complications.' Coni has held office since 1978, and feels that of all the changes he has made, the most pleasing is that he has strengthened the financial structure of the Regatta without changing the atmosphere.

He measures the success of the event strictly in terms of the quality of the competition rather than in the number of entries. 'Contrary to popular myth, the international flavour of Henley until a decade or two ago was very much the exception rather than the rule. But we can now watch a programme of racing, like the one in 1987, where nearly all the winners of the open events were Olympic or World Gold medallists.'

Peter Coni does recognise that his determination to encourage the participation of the very top names on the world stage tends to frighten most of the home crews into the lower, closed events. But he would hate to sacrifice the spectacle of current world stars like the

Canadian and Russian quads racing the final of the Queen Mother Cup, or Steve Redgrave and Andy Holmes rowing the Russian World Champions, the Pimenov brothers, to a standstill in the Goblets. What a tragedy to lose the presence of legendary performers like Peter-Michael Kolbe, the West German multi-world champion, in the Diamond Sculls.

He also gets exasperated by the continual sniping of the press, eager to convey an image of 'Hooray Henry lager lout toffs packed into an elitist Enclosure', which is simply inaccurate. Most of the Stewards' members, he insists firmly, are now current athletes or former Henley competitors who have an expert and passionate involvement in the proceedings out on the water. Like everything else, the world of British rowing has matured and moved on.

The problems he has faced during his chairmanship have been legion, but with a dry wit, a tough hand and a staff he clearly adores he has dealt with them all, and survived a heart attack into the bargain. His will be a hard act to follow.

What Henley Means

The glory of Henley, like Ascot, Trooping the Colour and all those other uniquely British events, is that it proves to the English that they still know how to run a show better than almost anyone else in the world and that people will come from all corners to watch us do it. It gives us a chance to show off; after all, rowing as a sport did start here.

For the oarsmen themselves, those who have raced in the past and since retired as well as those who are still competing, the Regatta provides five glorious days – come rain or shine – when they are centre stage. They can, without guilt or shame, indulge in memories, catch up with old friends, watch some high-class racing, and perhaps supply some of it themselves.

In 75 races over 25 years of competing at Henley, whether winning medals or just getting through a round or two, the Regatta has always held for me a thrill as great as (if very different from) a World Championships final or racing on the international regatta circuit.

The respectful, almost mystical quiet at the start next to Temple Island as you line up,

waiting for the order to 'go'; looking back over your shoulder away up the narrow course between the booms to the far-distant church beyond the finish; wishing your crewmates 'good luck'; the last deep breaths as the seconds count down; the tight coiled tension as the umpire rises to his feet and raises his flag; the sudden muscular release and explosion into action; the sense of close hand-to-hand combat with your opponents as you try to break them at the Barrier or failing that at Fawley or, God forbid if the battle should be so closely fought, after Remenham and the Mile; and then along the Enclosures with the shouts and cheers increasing inexorably to a roar as you approach the line.

The crowd is on top of you at Henley, not in some distant grandstand set back from a broad six-lane causeway. The adrenalin boost is unforgettable and the desire to repeat it hard to resist. This is rowing's equivalent of Wimbledon's Centre Court, of Wembley on Cup Final day. That is why the old dogs come back again and again. Just to be there, in that deep valley between the hills, is to get yet another shot of that exhilarating high. Henley Royal Regatta is a photographer's paradise, although professional practitioners are forbidden to roam the grounds inside the Stewards' Enclosure. To record such unique scenes of the English at play and the exotic nature of their style and their manners, it is left to the racegoer with a keen eye and a sharp wit like Roger Clark to bear witness.

Henley – the Regatta is a documentary in stills. The pictures are loosely arranged in sequence to represent a day in the life of the Regatta. Crowds arrive to watch morning preparations as crews limber up. Then follow racing, lunch, more racing, tea, finals, celebrations, prize-giving and the end – including extraordinary scenes in 1988 when heavy rain transformed the Stewards' Enclosure into a mud bath. The events recorded took place between 1983 and 1988, with a break in 1987 when Roger Clark was photographing in Russia. The pictures emphasise traditional aspects of the Regatta, but they do more. They capture Henley at its peak in the 1980s. The rowing commentator John Snagge once described Henley as 'a junior Ascot'. It has now come of age.

© 1989 Daniel Topolski

Nonchalant elegance of a
Henley regular.

Boathouses of Fisherman's Walk above the finish seen from the Photographers' Box.

W arming up and checking through the equipment before going afloat. Part ritual, part necessity, it settles nerves in the hour before the race.

S nap! Hats and stripes.
Meticulous dressing-up is *de
rigueur* for those who come to
parade.

Last–minute instructions to the cox.

Boat tents and launching pontoons viewed from the steps of the Press Box sited a few yards above the finish, in mid-stream and connected to the shore by a narrow gang plank. *Eva*, the Victorian launch in the foreground, was the first steam-powered launch to appear at Henley, in 1874; until then umpires had followed the races on horseback.

Henley-watching need not be
done only from the Stewards'
Enclosure. Choose your vintage and
select your vantage point.

L unch can be as tiring for the
spectators as the rowing is for
the athletes.

M ark Dunstan, Oxford
University oarsman, 1986.

M̲ental preparation for the race. His trusty shell slung above helps to concentrate his thoughts.

Local schoolboys man the Regatta entrance gates, checking for badges and improperly dressed visitors. A skirt too short, a top shirt button undone or a loosely knotted tie is enough to incur their wrath.

The Press Box gangplank. Henley Steward Alan Burrough, who with his wife Rosie donated the funds to secure Temple Island at the Regatta start, preparing to go afloat in his stylish launch *Bamboozle*.

Allan Green, No. 5 with the
Syracuse crew from America,
1988.

A Princeton oarsman collects
the lightweight Concept II
oars he and his crewmates will use
in their race. This American-made blade has replaced traditional wood
as the oarsman's favourite pulling
instrument.

Final adjustments on the bank outside the boat tents. In the background, Thomi Keller, President of FISA – the international rowing federation – and a Henley Steward, talks with the Australian national coach Reinhold Batschi.

Pensive member of the 1985
Salisbury school eight, one of
the strongest and most regular
American visitors for the Princess
Elizabeth Cup.

S ome things about Henley never
 change.

G oing afloat. The lull before the
storm – an unusually quiet
moment on the first day of racing.

Motorised boating must not make waves. Officials keep launch speeds to a minimum to protect racing crews from unsettling washes.

G rim-faced coach Tony
Mitchell, former oarsman
with Oxford's reserve crew Isis,
prepares to send his schoolboy crew
out for their race.

V iew from the Press Box. Half
an hour to go: the 1985
Harvard crew, stroked by Andy
Sudduth, wait for the regatta course
to clear before they head down to
the start for their race.

The Enclosure opposite the hole in the wall; the traditional 'take her home' sprint mark for racing crews, a minute from the finishing line.

The start: a stakeboat boy holds on to the stern of a boat lining up before the 'go'. Instructions relayed through his headphones from the line judge on the bank tell him to wind in or out to bring the crews level.

The last gasp.

'Are you ready? Go!' Christopher Davidge, one of Oxford's most heroic oarsmen, international medallist, Olympian, FISA and British Olympic Association official and Henley Steward, prepares to start a race.

Time-keepers and race-recorders man the rear of the umpires' launches. David Chipp, Steward and former Editor-in-Chief of the Press Association, operates the stop watches, 'Bungie' Langton notes the details and Arnie Zarach, a photographer from Kingston, reports progress to the commentators at the finish.

Enjoying the race from the newly restored University College Boat Club barge, moored near Fawley, the half-way point, during the 1988 Regatta.

Isis Boat Club from Oxford and Imperial College London's coxless fours clash blades as they approach the finish of their Visitors' Cup semi-final. Isis, with future mutiny-afflicted President Donald Macdonald on board, was disqualified and Imperial College, stroked by future Cambridge Blue Guy Pooley, went on to win the 1985 event.

Defeat.

Carrying the eight into the boat
tents.

Disconsolate Molesey Boat
Club come off the water after
their race.

The oarsman's home from
home – he can spend more than
twenty hours a week in this space.

An alternative to formal lunch under canvas within the Stewards' Enclosure is the car park picnic. Some are unkempt and relaxed while others are grand, stylised Rolls-Royce affairs.

E ven the most mundane
information signs have a
traditional look about them.

I nside the Enclosure·the band (usually the Grenadier Guards) plays favourite classics throughout the day, ending with the National Anthem at which the assembled racegoers come to attention. Out on the water the more patriotic oarsmen stand up in their boats.

Fashion on parade.

Princeton's elegant informality in the crews' amenity tent is strictly forbidden within the Stewards' Enclosure. British schoolboys manage less sartorial style.

Early morning and early evening – or just before and after feeding times – is when loyal supporters can seize the chance to get close to the water's edge.

Preparing for a hard afternoon's
race-watching.

Pangbourne's finest.

T his tree used to carry the score sheet and provide the most convenient meeting spot for Regatta-goers. It has since been chopped down and a sapling planted in its place in memory of Henley Steward Kenneth Payne.

Defeat has its compensations.

F ashion parade inside the
Enclosure; vintage car parade
outside.

Trophies are on display during the five days of racing. Many competitors believe that to see the cup before the finals are over spells bad luck.

View from the Photographers'
Box on the finishing line.
Motor launches and cabin cruisers
are allowed to pass slowly up and
down the open channel of the
Henley stretch outside the boomed
race course. The river police
maintain order.

A Harvard man. Regular Henley competitors who rarely fail to take home a coveted trophy.

Emmanuel College Cambridge
man sporting traditional
Henley blazer.

Open to all. Picnicking, sunbathing (and boozing) on the grass outside the boat tents was one of the greatest pleasures for non Stewards' Enclosure Regatta-goers. Now access to the boat tent area is restricted to allow competitors to prepare undisturbed, save by family, close friends, journalists and ticket holders!

E wart Martin (*centre*) and his colleagues have been keeping the crews fully informed for many years.

B etter luck next year?

T emple Island, bought in 1987
for the Regatta's use, marks the
start of the race. The umpire is
Chairman Peter Coni.

The finish.

A clear run. An umpire raises his flag to signify the end of the race as the rival fours converge on the Bucks side of the course.

Leander's four beyond the finish line. Leander Club, 100 yards above the Regatta Enclosures below Henley Bridge, is the world's most prestigious rowing club.

Through to another round?

E_{xhaustion.}

H^{as he won?}

The *Empress of India* steams up and down the course providing alternative entertainment to the band in the Stewards' Enclosure for guests both on board and onshore.

View down the race course from the Press Box. The *Guardian* correspondent Christopher Dodd (*left*) sits behind Geoffrey Page of the *Telegraph*, who occupies his regular Henley seat.

Hats are to Henley-goers what
scarves are to football fans.

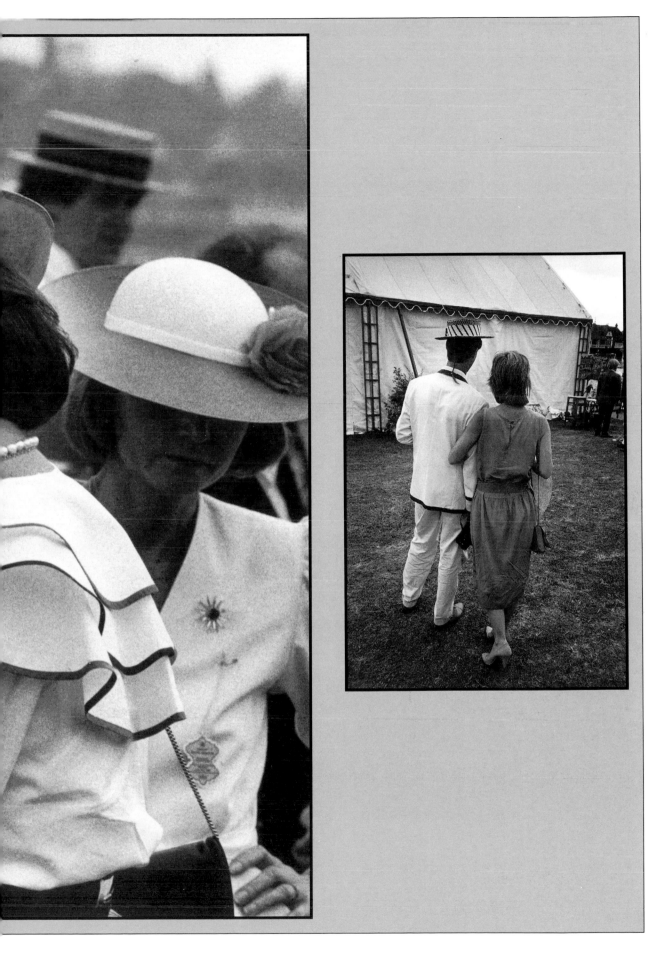

Fashionable pigtail constrained
by compulsory formality.

A crew observed – and clearly
on its feet and under no
pressure.

The Leander raft.

Princeton defeated. The losing crew always shows the greatest distress – especially when they have travelled over 3,000 miles to take part.

Looking forward to the next round. Radley College carry their boat ashore.

Crew members and coaches discover the results of the Henley draw, posted on the notice boards alongside the competitors' enquiry office.

Poplar Point, six strokes from the
finish.

Harvard in repose.

Eye-catcher.

Trumpeters take a break before
heralding the arrival of royalty
for the prize-giving.

The coffee bar next to the bandstand inside the Stewards' Enclosure.

Time-keeper Alan Burrough, Henley Steward, Temple Island benefactor and former Chairman of Beefeaters Gin, prepares to go afloat with the umpire. In the centre foreground Alan Mays–Smith waits to officiate on the following race.

One of the finest ever victories in the Grand Challenge Cup. The British Olympic eight defeats the Australian national crew by a foot in 1988. The crews finished fourth and fifth in Seoul.

R oyalty in the rain. The
umpire and Chairman of the
Regatta, Peter Coni, hosts the
Princess Royal watching the race

opposite. Coach of the British
victors Terry O'Neill sits behind
Princess Anne.

Willie Ross, sometime cox for Thames Rowing Club and coach to the Elizabethan Boat Club, collects his crews' oars from the landing pontoon.

Harvard celebrate their 1985 triumph in the Grand Challenge Cup in traditional style – the cox is about to follow her crewmates into the water.

Harvard collect their prize from
Prince Andrew, and share the
champagne in their trophy, the
Grand Challenge Cup.

Henley regulars.

The day's racing is over for
Pangbourne college oarsman.

Oarsman from Kent School,
USA.

Entrance to the Stewards'
Enclosure and the badge
collection office.

O undle school crew mates
commiserate? celebrate? try
to forget?

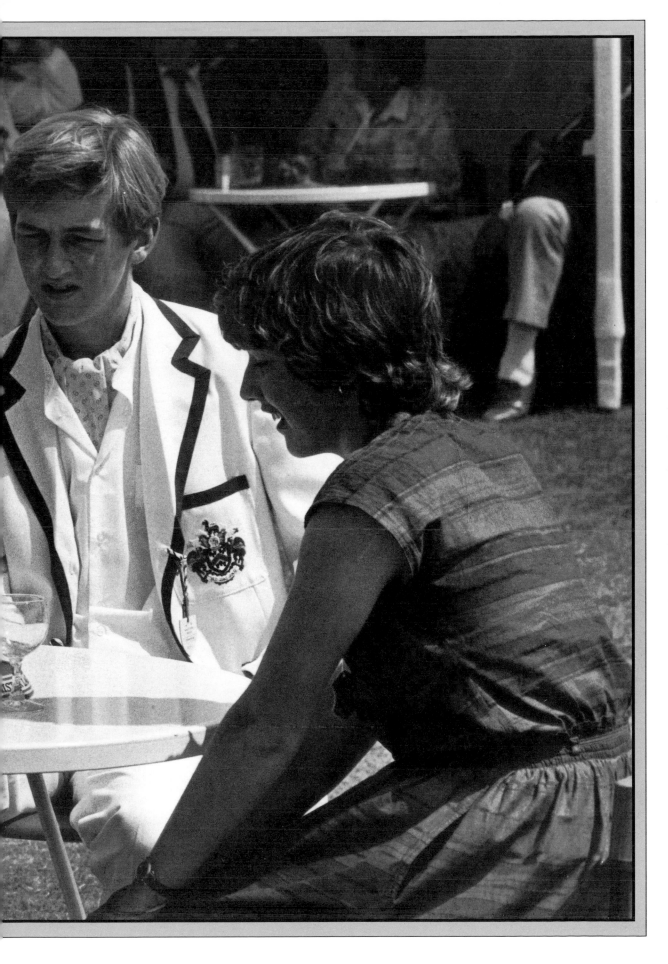

R ain never stops play.

A member of the Canadian coxed four, winners of the Prince Philip Cup, displays his medal, 1988.

Cambridge coach Donald Legget is well prepared for all weather conditions.

Oarsman from Temple
College, USA.

Although rain reduced the
Stewards' Enclosure to a mud
bath in 1988, the end-of-regatta
celebrations continued unimpaired.

R egatta's end.